English Skills 3

Published by Collins
An imprint of HarperCollins*Publishers*
77–85 Fulham Palace Road
Hammersmith
London
W6 8JB

Browse the complete Collins catalogue at
www.collinseducation.com

© HarperCollins*Publishers* Limited 2011, on behalf of the author

First published in 2006 by Folens Limited.

ISBN-13: 978-0-00-743720-7

All rights reserved. No part of this publication may be reproduced, stored in a retrieval system, or transmitted in any form or by any means, electronic, mechanical, photocopying, recording or otherwise, without the prior written permission of the Publisher or a licence permitting restricted copying in the United Kingdom issued by the Copyright Licensing Agency Ltd, 90 Tottenham Court Road, London W1T 4LP.

British Library Cataloguing in Publication Data
A catalogue record for this publication is available from the British Library.

Every effort has been made to trace copyright holders and to obtain their permission for the use of copyright material. The authors and publishers will gladly receive any information enabling them to rectify any error or omission in subsequent editions.

Editor: Geraldine Sowerby
Layout artist: Patricia Hollingsworth
Illustrations: Tony Randell
Cover design: Martin Cross
Editorial consultant: Helen Whittaker

Printed and bound in China.

Contents

Reading	Volcanoes	4
Activities		5
Phonics	Initial and Final Blends	6
Grammar	Capital Letters	7
Writing		8
Language	Using Words	9
Reading	Marty Mouse and Cousin Jerry	10
Activities		11
Phonics	Final Blends: 'ck and 'ing'	12
Grammar	Capital Letters	13
Writing		14
Language	Using Words	15
Reading	Witch Goes Shopping	16
Activities		17
Phonics	Magic 'E'	18
Grammar	Full Stops and Question Marks	19
Writing		20
Language	Using Words	21
Reading	Goldenhair	22
Activities		23
Phonics	Vowel Diagraphs: 'ai' and 'oa'	24
Grammar	Singular and Plural	25
Writing		26
Language	Using Words	27
Reading	The Olympic Games	28
Activities		29
Phonics	Vowel Diagraphs: 'ea and 'ee'	30
Grammar	Singular and Plural	31
Writing		32
Language	Using Words	33
Reading	Honesty is the Best Policy	34
Activities		35
Phonics	Vowel Diagraphs: 'oo' and 'ew'	36
Grammar	Alphabetical Order	37
Writing		38
Language	Using Words	39
Reading	Snowflake	40
Activities		41
Phonics	Consonant Diagraphs: 'ph', 'wh' and 'th'	42
Grammar	Alphabetical Order	43
Writing		44
Language	Using Words	45
Reading	The Big Fish	46
Activities		47
Phonics	Three-letter Blends: 'spl' and 'spr'	48
Grammar	Comparative and Superlative	49
Writing		50
Language	Using Words	51
Reading	The First Lighthouse	52
Activities		53
Phonics	Three-letter Blends: 'scr and 'str'	54
Grammar	Nouns	55
Writing		56
Language	Using Words	57
Reading	The Tall Giraffe	58
Activities		59
Phonics	Soft 'c' and hard 'c'	60
Grammar	Nouns	61
Writing		62
Language	Using Words	63
Reading	Bell the Cat	64
Activities		65
Phonics	Soft 'g'and Hard 'g'	66
Grammar	Verbs	67
Writing		68
Language	Using Words	69
Reading	The Fairies	70
Activities		71
Phonics	Silent Letters: 'k' and 'w'	72
Grammar	Verbs	73
Writing		74
Language	Using Words	75
Reading	The Shy Kingfisher	76
Activities		77
Phonics	Root Words and Compound Words	78
Grammar	Adjectives	79
Writing		80
Language	Using Words	81
Reading	The Salmon of Knowledge	82
Activities		83
Phonics	Syllables	84
Grammar	Adjectives	85
Writing		86
Language	Using Words	87
Reading	Dolphins	88
Activities		89
Phonics	Syllables	90
Grammar	Confusing Words	91
Writing		92
Language	Using Words	93
Reading	Strange Friends	94
Activities		95
Reading	If I Knew	96

Reading

 A Read the text.

Volcanoes

A volcano is a hole in the Earth's surface. When a volcano erupts, lava (melted rock), hot gases, rock and ash are thrown into the air. Most volcanoes are mountains. This is because the rock that the volcano blasts out every time it erupts builds up over thousands of years.

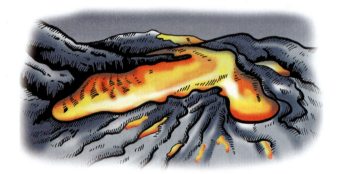

There are volcanoes under the sea as well as on land. The lava from eruptions under the sea slowly raises the level of the seabed. This is how volcanic islands, like Hawaii, are formed.

Volcanic eruptions have caused some of the worst disasters in history. Over two thousand years ago Mount Vesuvius in Italy erupted, burying the town of Pompeii and killing thousands of people. About one hundred and twenty years ago, the eruption of Krakatoa in Indonesia killed even more people. The clouds of ash blasted out changed the world's weather for the next five years.

The word 'volcano' comes from Vulcan, the Ancient Roman god of fire. The Romans believed he lived underneath the volcanic island of Vulcano, which lies just off the coast of Italy.

Activities

A Answer these questions.

1. What is a volcano?

2. What is lava?

3. Where is Mount Vesuvius?

4. When did Krakatoa erupt?

5. For how long did the eruption of Krakatoa change the world's weather?

6. Where does the word 'volcano' come from?

B Write **true** or **false**.

1. When a volcano erupts, nothing is thrown into the air.

2. Most volcanoes are mountains.

3. There are volcanoes under the sea.

4. Mount Vesuvius is in Spain.

5. Krakatoa is in Indonesia.

6. Vulcan was the Ancient Greek god of fire.

Phonics

Initial and Final Blends

A Copy the words. Write in the missing letters.

| pl | gl | pr | fl | cr | dr | br | fr |

- c r ab
- __ um
- __ um
- __ ick
- __ ag
- __ am
- __ ass
- __ og

B Write the correct word.

- bank / tank → tank
- dent / belt
- monk / milk
- tent / sent
- mask / task
- test / nest
- sunk / sink
- camp / lamp

Grammar

Capital Letters

 A Write the correct word.

We use **capital letters:**

1. At the start of a _____. (set, school, sentence)
2. For a person's _____. (neck, name, nose)
3. For the name of a _____. (wet day, weekday, washday)
4. For the name of a _____. (mouth, month, match)
5. For the name of a _____. (plate, plot, place)
6. For the word _____. (oh, and, I)
7. For special _____. (days, ducks, numbers)

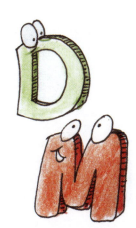

 B Write these sentences correctly.

1. i will travel to egypt on tuesday.

2. my friend's name is paul.

3. june comes between may and july.

4. eid is in february.

5. mehmet and i are going to belfast in may.

6. mum and meg will be in rome until easter sunday.

7. divali is in november.

8. tom and i met jafar in ethiopia at christmas.

Writing

A Copy and complete this 'fact file' about yourself.

Name: _____

Name of school: _____

Class: _____

Teacher's name: _____

Age: _____

Date of birth: _____

Male or Female: _____

Country of birth: _____

Colour of hair: _____

Colour of eyes: _____

Height: _____

Brothers: _____

Sisters: _____

Pets: _____

Hobbies: _____

Favourite book: _____

Favourite TV programme: _____

Favourite colour: _____

Favourite actor: _____

Language

Using Words

 A Write the correct word.

1. The _____ (rabbit, bear, tiger) has a long tail.
2. The _____ (lion, cat, rabbit) has a short tail.
3. The _____ (rabbit, mouse, squirrel) has a bushy tail.
4. The _____ (horse, deer, hare) has a long tail.
5. The _____ (mouse, sheep, kangaroo) has a short tail.
6. The _____ (lamb, goat, fox) has a bushy tail.

B Write the correct word.

| white | tame | fast | heavy | large | thin | sweet | soft |

1. The mouse is *small* but the elephant is _____ .
2. The snail is *slow* but the hare is _____ .
3. The lion is *wild* but the sheepdog is _____ .
4. The feather is *light* but the rock is _____ .
5. The stone is *hard* but the jelly is _____ .
6. The penguin is *fat* but the greyhound is _____ .
7. The lemon is *bitter* but the sugar is _____ .
8. The coal is *black* but the snow is _____ .

 C Write the correct word.

| team | pride | litter | nest | herd | pack | troop | flock | school | pod |

1. A _____ of mice.
2. A _____ of wolves.
3. A _____ of elephants.
4. A _____ of kittens.
5. A _____ of lions.
6. A _____ of horses.
7. A _____ of cod.
8. A _____ of monkeys.
9. A _____ of birds.
10. A _____ of whales.

Reading

A Read the story.

Marty Mouse and Cousin Jerry

Marty Mouse lived in a large house in the city. One day, he visited his country cousin, Jerry, who lived alone in a cosy nest near a wood.

Seeds and plants were all Jerry ever had to eat. Marty did not enjoy that kind of food. He loved to nibble cakes, buns and biscuits. After a few days with Jerry, he decided to return to his city house.

"Why not return with me for a holiday," said Marty to his cousin, as he packed his suitcase for home.

"That would be wonderful," said Jerry, as he clapped his tiny paws. "Let us go at once."

That night Marty and Jerry set off on their long journey. At last, tired and hungry, they arrived at the big house. They squeezed through a tiny hole that led into the kitchen.

Jerry ran across the floor and soon found a cream bun. "This is lovely," said the happy mouse. "I'll never go back to the country."

Just then, Marty stood still and listened. He saw two big, round eyes staring at him. "Run, Jerry run!" he squeaked. "Here comes Leo, the cat!"

With one jump, Marty was inside the hole in the cupboard. Jerry rushed after him, but the cat's large paw scratched his tail as he fled into the hole.

"Well! well!" laughed Marty. "That was close! Hungry Leo nearly had you for his dinner."

Poor little Jerry was crying.

"That wicked cat bit off the end of my tail. It will never again be nice and curly."

"I'm sorry," replied Marty. "But when you live in the city you must be quick or a hungry cat will eat you."

"Oh dear!" squeaked Jerry, who was scared.

"I am sorry I came here at all. It is much better to live a long life in the country than a short one in the city. Goodbye, Marty. It was kind of you to invite me to the city, but I am going home at once."

So, back to the country went Jerry leaving his cousin, Marty, behind in the big city to play games of 'hide and seek' with the cats.

Activities

A **Write true or false.**

1. Marty Mouse lived in the country. _____
2. Jerry ate seeds and plants. _____
3. Marty invited Jerry to his house in the city. _____
4. Jerry found a cream biscuit. _____
5. The cat's name was Leo. _____
6. The cat bit the end of Jerry's nose. _____
7. Jerry decided to go home at once. _____
8. Marty decided to go home with Jerry. _____

B **Write the missing words.**

hungry chased Marty country Jerry house back Mouse Leo

Marty _____ lived in a big _____ in the city. His cousin _____ lived in the _____. Jerry went to visit _____.

Jerry was _____ by a big _____ cat called _____.

He decided to go _____ home to his house in the country.

C **How many small words can you make from 'squeaked'?**

_____   _____
_____   _____
_____   _____
_____   _____

11

Phonics

Final Blends: 'ck and 'ing'

 A Write the correct word.

 B Choose the correct word.

1. I lost my diamond _____. (wing, king, ring)
2. Can you _____ (bring, thing, sting) your umbrella?
3. My arm is in a _____. (swing, sling, sting)
4. I was _____ (winning, running, robbing) too fast and fell.
5. The farmer is _____ (shouting, hearing, shearing) the sheep.
6. My mum is _____ (calling, falling, coming) me.

Grammar

Capital Letters

A Write the word that needs a capital letter.

1. dog, house, pencil, august   _____
2. grass, tom, mouse, truck   _____
3. desk, flower, squirrel, paris   _____
4. divali, woman, dentist, rabbit   _____
5. tree, ramadan, book, glass   _____
6. chair, tiger, tuesday, baby   _____

B Write these sentences correctly.

1. i fed the calves in their pen.

   _____

2. i am sure i was first to see the eagle.

   _____

3. the school will be closed on saturday and sunday.

   _____

4. we go to school from monday to friday.

   _____

5. in england the summer months are june, july and august.

   _____

6. my friends and i have fun at eid.

   _____

Writing

A Write a story. Use the words below to help you write.

> birthday   auntie arrived   surprise   present
> fluffy, white rabbit   cute and cuddly   friendly and playful
> named it   built a hutch   soft straw   water
> feed of lettuce and carrots   nibbled happily
> clean out each day   playing in the back garden
> hopping and skipping   take good care of

A New Pet

_____
_____
_____
_____
_____
_____

Language

Using Words

A Write the correct word.

1. A wild rabbit lives in a _____. (den, burrow, bush)
2. A rabbit has a covering of _____. (wool, hair, fur)
3. A rabbit eats _____. (fish, vegetables, paper)
4. A rabbit is smaller than a _____. (fox, mouse, rat)
5. A rabbit cannot _____. (leap, jump, fly)
6. A young rabbit _____. (barks, brays, squeals)
7. A tame rabbit lives in a _____. (nest, hole, hutch)
8. A rabbit is a _____. (reptile, bird, mammal)
9. A wild rabbit is very _____. (tame, tiny, shy)

B Which of these animals have long or short tails?

giraffe   hare   deer   goat   sheep   squirrel   fox
bear   monkey   kangaroo

Long-tailed animals	Short-tailed animals

C Find and write down the 'odd one out' in each row.

1. black, blame, blue, block, clown   _____
2. chicken, chocolate, stamp, chimney   _____
3. sheep, piano, shop, shell, ship   _____
4. thief, think, snake, thing, thin   _____
5. flower, frog, flock, flat, flag   _____
6. slipper, stick, slug, sling, sleep   _____

Reading

A Read the poem.

Witch Goes Shopping

Witch rides off
Upon her broom
Finds a space
To park it.
Takes a shiny shopping cart
Into the supermarket.
Smacks her lips and reads
The list of things she needs:
'Six bats' wings
Worms in brine
Ears of toads
Eight or nine.
Slugs and bugs
Snake skins dried
Buzzard innards
Pickled, fried.'
Witch takes herself
From shelf to shelf
Cackling all the while.
Up and down and up and down and
In and out each aisle.
Out come cans and cartons
Tumbling to the floor.
'This,' says Witch, now all a-twitch
'Is a crazy store.
I CAN'T FIND A SINGLE THING
I AM LOOKING FOR!'

Lilian Moore

Activities

A Answer these questions.

1. Where was Witch going?
2. How many ears of toads was she looking for?
3. What type of snake skins were on her list?
4. What type of buzzard innards did she want?
5. Why did she become angry?

B Match the words any way you like. Write the new ingredients in the trolley.

fried	snail shells	twelve	bats' legs
boiled	snake tongues	baked	spiders' webs
pickled	frogs' legs	nine	worm skins
grilled	tadpole jelly	barbequed	buzzard claws
seven	snail slime	tinned	fly's wings

boiled tadpole jelly

17

Phonics

Magic 'E'

A Copy this magic 'E' crossword onto squared paper. Fill in the missing letters.

Across
1. A piece of rock.
3. A ball with a map of the world on it.
5. Unscramble the letters: e t k s a.
9. A box where bees live.
10. The opposite to black.
12. A woman on her wedding day.
13. A long reptile with no legs.
15. A flat dish for food.

Down
1. Unscramble the letters: p a s h e.
2. You smell with it.
4. Can face danger with no fear.
6. Unscramble the letters: r t b i e.
7. A place with no sunlight.
8. To cut off hair with a razor.
11. The opposite of wild.
14. A toy that flies on a string.

Grammar

Full Stops and Question Marks

A Write full stops or question marks at the end of each sentence.

1. What class are you in
2. My name is Jamila
3. I have a pet rabbit
4. Which pencil is yours
5. Who broke the window
6. I have brown hair
7. Who owns this hat
8. Did you go to bed early
9. The train arrived late
10. Do you have my ruler
11. Where is the new teacher
12. How old are you

B Write questions for these answers.

1. _____ She is eight years old.
2. _____ School starts at nine o'clock.
3. _____ It is his book.
4. _____ The nurse came to the school.
5. _____ She cried because she was sick.
6. _____ The pigeon is on the roof.
7. _____ The front wheel of the car fell off.
8. _____ They live four kilometres from Beijing.
9. _____ The train arrived at noon.
10. _____ Money is kept in a bank.

C Unscramble these sentences. Write full stops or question marks.

1. thick lay the snow on ground the
2. meet to we agreed the at shops
3. late you why are morning every
4. you did what for have dinner
5. fog a thick covered London yesterday
6. be you what will up dressing as

Writing

A Write a story. Use the words bellow to help you write.

> in the park   playing 'hide and seek'
> hidden in a bush   sound of footsteps   whispers
> a mean-looking man and woman   the man was
> and wore   the woman   a brown bag   scared
> as quiet as a   stuffed the bag under   hurried away
> waited a moment   crept   reward
> pulled out the bag   opened   police station

The Stolen Money

_____
_____
_____
_____
_____

Language

Using Words

A Write the correct word.

1. A _____ (fox, camel, goat) has a hump on its back.
2. A _____ (rat, mouse, giraffe) has a long neck.
3. A _____ (lion, sheep, rabbit) has a long mane.
4. A _____ (monkey, dog, fox) is a good climber.
5. A _____ (duck, horse, bear) growls when it is angry.
6. A _____ (duck, robin, penguin) cannot fly.
7. A _____ (monkey, ape, tiger) is a member of the cat family.
8. A _____ (goat, deer, seal) has flippers instead of legs.
9. An _____ (ant, elephant, owl) has tusks.
10. A _____ (swallow, robin, parrot) can talk.

B Write the missing words.

| young | hard | gardener | leaves | slime | food |
| shell | shy | backs | legs | snails | build |

The Snail

What funny things _____ are! They have no _____, and yet they can travel. They have houses, and yet they did not _____ them. They can carry their houses on their _____, and yet not be tired.

The snail is very _____. If anyone comes near, it will hide in its _____. If you touch a snail, it will go into its _____. It uses feelers instead of hands. The snail feels for its _____ with them.

This is a _____ snail. Its shell is not very _____ yet. The _____ does not like snails. They eat the green _____. A snail has tiny teeth. It uses them to grind its food. Have you seen the trail of silver _____ which the snail leaves behind as it crawls along?

Reading

A Read the story.

Goldenhair

Once upon a time, a golden-haired girl lost her way in a forest. She ran this way and that until she could run no further. She lay down on the grass and soon she fell asleep.

Suddenly, out stepped two little dwarfs. They stood on either side of the girl and watched and waited.

At last she awoke. She was surprised to see the little dwarfs, but they smiled at her in a friendly way.

"If you let me cut off your golden hair," said one dwarf, " I shall give you a gold ring."

But the girl said, "No! No! I shall not give you even a lock of my hair. I was born with it and I must keep it."

The other dwarf said, "If you let me cut off your golden hair, I shall give you a doll's kitchen, with all the dishes made of pure silver."

Again, the girl shook her head. "I was born with my hair and I am keeping it," she said.

The first dwarf then spoke. "If you let me cut off your ringlets, you will have a little bird which will lay a golden egg every day."

But the girl shook her head once more.

"Listen to me," said one of the dwarfs. "You have a brother at home who is very ill. I have a little bag of special tea. If you boil it and give it to your brother, he will be well again."

The girl clapped her hands. "Quick! Quick!" she cried. "Give me the bag of tea, please!"

"Only if you will let me cut off your golden hair," said the dwarf.

"Yes! Yes! Cut it off quickly and let me run home to my sick brother," said the girl.

But the little dwarf said, "I am glad that you love your sick brother so much. Here is the special tea and you can also keep your golden hair, because you are so good and kind. Now hurry home as fast as you can."

The dwarfs led the girl to the edge of the wood and showed her the shortest way home.

The girl ran home as fast as she could, carrying the bag of tea in her hand.

Activities

A Answer these questions.

1. Where did the girl get lost?
2. Why did she fall asleep?
3. What did she see when she woke up?
4. What did one dwarf want from her?
5. What reward did he offer her?
6. Why did she refuse?
7. Who was sick in the girl's home?
8. Why was she willing to give away her golden hair?
9. Why did the dwarf not take it from her?
10. How did she find her way out of the wood?

B Write the missing word.

1. f _ _ _ _ _

2. r _ _ _

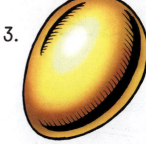
3. g _ _ _ _ _ e _ _

4. d _ _ _ _

5. b _ _ _ _ _ _

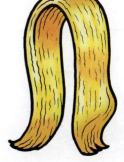
6. g _ _ _ _ _ h _ _ _

Phonics

Vowel Diagraphs: 'ai' and 'oa'

A Write the correct word.

1. A tiger has a long _____ (train, tail, sail).
2. A _____ (snail, train, stain) has its house on its back.
3. The snail left a _____ (train, snail, trail) of slime.
4. There were puddles after the _____ (pain, rain, rail).
5. The ship can _____ (snail, stain, sail) across the water.
6. I have a _____ (pail, pain, paint) in my foot.
7. The _____ (brain, mail, stool) has only three legs.

B Write the correct word.

gloat / goat	load / toad	coat / coal	foal / float
goat / goal	boast / boat	toast / soap	shoal / road
boast / toast	coast / roast	float / stoat	moan / moat

Grammar

Singular and Plural

| Singular means one | Plural means more than one |

A Write these in the plural.

Singular	Plural	Singular	Plural
tree		flower	
book		finger	
animal		poet	
river		battle	
game		apple	
girl		rabbit	
table		chair	
car		pencil	

B Add **s** or **es** to these words.

1. One girl but two _____ .
2. One fox but two _____ .
3. One watch but two _____ .
4. One bush but two _____ .
5. One class but two _____ .
6. One star but two _____ .
7. One witch but two _____ .
8. One thrush but two _____ .
9. One miss but two _____ .
10. One bone but two _____ .
11. One head but two _____ .
12. One wish but two _____ .
13. One box but two _____ .
14. One dish but two _____ .
15. One tree but two _____ .

Writing

A Write the story. Use the words bellow to help you write.

sleepless night   awake   felt sick   bad cough
terrible headache   pain   my father   stay in bed
no appetite   fever   rang the doctor   arrived   examined
bottle of medicine   five days   much improved

The Day I Was Sick

Language

Using Words

A Choose the correct word.

1. A cat has a coat of _____. (wool, fur, feathers)
2. A cat is _____. (a bird, an animal, an insect)
3. A cat likes to eat _____. (corn, fish, snails)
4. A cat has no _____. (horns, whiskers, tail)
5. A young cat is called a _____. (cub, pup, kitten)
6. A cat likes to chase _____. (mice, dogs, sheep)
7. A happy cat _____. (barks, purrs, roars)
8. A cat has a long _____. (nose, tail, ear)

B Write the missing words.

| animals | cubs | zebras | hunting | neck | Jungle |
| dangerous | strong | pride | groups | Africa | |

Lions live in the great plains of _____. They travel around in small _____. A family of lions is called a _____.

The male lion is big and _____. He is called the King of the _____. He has a brown mane round his _____. The lioness has no mane. She is smaller than the lion, but more active. She does most of the _____. She kills deer and _____. She takes good care of her _____. The lioness teaches them to hunt when they are young.

Lions are shy _____ and usually avoid people. Sometimes, an old lion will turn man-eater and then it is very _____.

Reading

A Read the text.

The Olympic Games

The Olympic Games, which is held every four years, is the most important athletic competition in the world. During the Olympic Games, the best athletes in the world compete against each other. More than one billion people across the world watch the Olympic Games on television.

The Olympic Games started in Ancient Greece and was held for over a thousand years. The modern games began in 1896. The organizers wanted to encourage peace and friendship between the countries of the world and they also wanted young people to be fit and healthy.

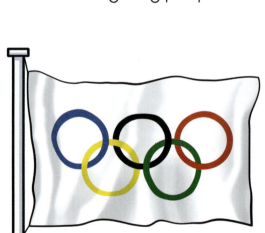

During the opening ceremony, the athletes from Greece march into the stadium first, in honour of the original games. The athletes from other countries enter in alphabetical order. The athletes of the host country enter last, and then the Olympic flag is raised.

The symbol on the Olympic flag is made up of five coloured rings that represent the continents of Africa, Asia, Australia, Europe, and North and South America. The flag of every country competing in the games has at least one of these five colours in it.

The most important part of the opening ceremony is the lighting of the Olympic flame. Days before, a fire is lit in Olympia, Greece, by using a mirror to collect the rays of the sun. Many runners take turns carrying the flame from Greece to the site of the games. The flame burns throughout the games, but it is put out during the closing ceremony.

Activities

A Write the correct word.

1. The Olympic Games are held every _____ (three, four, five) years.
2. The Olympic Games started in Ancient _____. (Egypt, Rome, Greece)
3. During the opening ceremony, the athletes from _____ (Greece, Italy, the host country) enter the stadium first.
4. The five coloured rings represent five _____. (oceans, continents, seasons)
5. The colours of the rings are blue, yellow, black, green and _____. (red, white, brown)
6. A fire is lit in _____. (Athens, Paris, Olympia)
7. The flame is carried by _____. (pigeons, runners, dogs)
8. The Olympic flame is put out during the _____ (opening, closing, flag) ceremony.

B Write true or false.

1. The ancient Olympic Games lasted for over a thousand years. _____
2. The modern games began in 1986. _____
3. The Olympic flag represents the continents of the world. _____
4. The most important part of the closing ceremony is the lighting of the Olympic flame. _____
5. The Olympic flame is put out during the opening ceremony. _____

C Unscramble these sentences.
Do not forget capital letters and full stops!

1. began the 1896 games in modern
2. is held the Olympic every Games four years
3. stadium the Greek athletes the first enter
4. during the games flame burns the Olympic

Phonics

Vowel Diagraphs: 'ea and 'ee'

 A Write the correct word.

beak / beat	team / meat	flea / leaf	tea / eat
beak / bean	dear / read	lead / leaf	flea / heal
seal / steam	steal / steam	dream / dear	cream / real

 B Write the missing ee word.

1. I'm going to Spain next _____ (wake, week, weed).
2. I can _____ (peck, pale, peel) this orange in one go.
3. I will _____ (meet, meat, meal) you at the bus stop.
4. I have to _____ (week, weed, weep) the garden.
5. The _____ (deer, reed, dear) is in the park.
6. I have _____ (been, bore, bone) waiting for you.
7. They had to _____ (flare, feel, flee) from the town.

Grammar

Singular and Plural

 A How do we get the plural of the words below?

> We change the f to v and add es.

Write the plural of the words in purple.

1. The hunter saw the **wolf**. _____
2. The butcher bought the **calf**. _____
3. The fan wore the **scarf**. _____
4. The insect fed on the **leaf**. _____
5. We ate the fish and the **loaf** of bread. _____
6. The shoemaker gave the present to the **elf**. _____
7. He cut the rope with the **knife**. _____
8. The carpenter repaired the **shelf**. _____

B Write these in the plural.

Singular +s	Plural	Singular +es	Plural
video	_____	potato	_____
banjo	_____	volcano	_____
piano	_____	hero	_____
photo	_____	echo	_____
dynamo	_____	tomato	_____
cuckoo	_____	tornado	_____
cello	_____	domino	_____
torso	_____	cargo	_____

 C Rewrite these sentences in the singular.

1. The rabbits ran into the fields. _____
2. I watched the robins on the branches. _____
3. The boys saw the cuckoos. _____
4. Finn burned his fingers and tasted the salmon. _____
5. The sheep ran when they saw the tornadoes. _____
6. The girls saw the videos on the shelves. _____

31

Writing

A Write a story. Use the words below to help you write.

> moonlit night   silent hills   prowling fox   lonely farmhouse
> sneaked around   small outhouse   sleeping hens
> slunk towards   crept under   snatched   hens
> noise and panic   ran quickly   fled   farmer awoke   stairs
> searched   no sign

The Hungry Fox

Language

Using Words

A Write the correct word.

1. As sly as a _____ (rat, fox, rabbit).
2. As blind as a _____ (rat, bat, cat).
3. As slow as a _____ (hare, fox, snail).
4. As gentle as a _____ (lamb, hawk, tiger).
5. As strong as an _____ (ox, horse, insect).
6. As swift as a _____ (robin, hawk, crow).
7. As hungry as a _____ (mouse, fox, wolf).
8. As brave as a _____ (monkey, deer, lion).
9. As wise as an _____ (eagle, owl, ostrich).
10. As busy as a _____ (elephant, bee, snail).

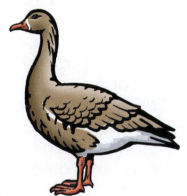

B Write the correct word.

| coop   stable   burrow   web   den   cave   hole   nest |

1. A fox lives in a _____ .
2. A wild rabbit lives in a _____ .
3. A spider lives in a _____ .
4. A wasp lives in a _____ .
5. A bat lives in a _____ .
6. A mouse lives in a _____ .
7. A hen lives in a _____ .
8. A horse lives in a _____ .

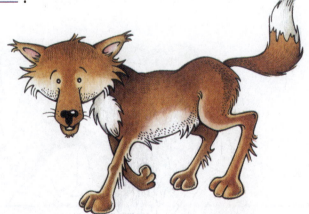

C Write the opposite.

1. black and _____
2. north and _____
3. float and _____
4. fat and _____
5. first and _____
6. strong and _____
7. sharp and _____
8. cold and _____

Reading

A Read the story.

Honesty is the Best Policy

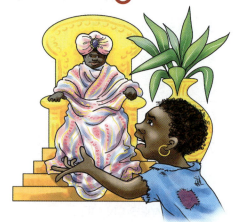

Long ago in Africa, a poor man worked for a farmer. He complained so much that the king heard about it.

"Why are you always complaining?" the king asked.

"However hard I work I never earn extra money. I shall always be poor," complained the man.

"But are you honest?" asked the king.

"Of course I am honest," replied the man.

"Then you will be rich," said the king. "Here are two bags. The little one is for you and the big one is for the farmer."

As he walked along, the man wondered why the king had given him the small bag when he was much poorer than the farmer. It wasn't fair. He thought of keeping the big bag for himself, but that would not be honest.

Just before he got to the farm he hid the big bag and took the small bag to the farmer. The farmer was pleased to get a present from the king. He opened the bag. It was full of gold!

The poor man ran back to the hiding place, shouting, "I'm rich!, I'm rich!"

But when he opened the bag it was full of seed.

Activities

A Answer these questions.

1. Why was the poor man always complaining?
2. What did the king say the poor man must do to become rich?
3. Which bag did the king give to the poor man?
4. Was the poor man happy with his gift?
5. Which sack did he give to the farmer?
6. What did the farmer find in his sack?
7. What was in the poor man's sack?
8. What would have happened if the poor man had been honest?

B Write **true** or **false**.

1. The story takes place in America.
2. The queen heard about the man's complaining.
3. The king gave the poor man three bags.
4. The little bag was for the poor man.
5. The big bag was for the king.
6. The poor man hid the small bag.
7. The small bag was full of seed.
8. The big bag was full of gold.

C How many small words can you make from 'complaining'?

Phonics

Vowel Diagraphs: 'oo' and 'ew'

 A Write the correct word.

 B Choose the correct **ew** word.

1. I need a _____ (dew, nest, new) copy.
2. We're having _____ (blew, stew, stop) for dinner.
3. I _____ (three, threw, through) the ball.
4. My dog tried to _____ (chair, chew, grew) my shoe.
5. The wind _____ (blue, blew, drew) across the _____ (dew, few, new).
6. There was no _____ (new, news, knew) of the _____ (crew, chew).

Grammar

Alphabetical Order

A B C D E F G H I J K L M N O P Q R S T U V W X Y Z

A Write the missing letters.

C _ E _ _ H _ _ K _ _

N O _ Q _ S _ U _ _ X

B Which letter comes earlier in the alphabet?

1. D or B
2. I or K
3. L or J
4. P or F
5. N or M
6. U or W
7. S or T
8. F or G
9. U or R
10. J or H
11. O or Q
12. C or E

C Write these letters in alphabetical order.

1. G R B T D _____
2. M O R N L _____
3. E A D L K _____
4. V X T U Y _____

D Write these lists in alphabetical order. Underline the first letter in each word.

1. eel, frog, dog
2. plate, knife, fork
3. jersey, football, referee
4. daisy, tulip, buttercup
5. hot, warm, cold, freezing
6. chair, bed, table, mirror
7. polish, clean, shine, brush
8. guitar, drum, piano, flute
9. leaf, branch, root, trunk
10. tie, shirt, jumper, cap
11. happy, sad, angry, worried, fearful
12. oak, sycamore, ash, elm, beech

Writing

A Write a story. Use the words below to help you write.

> spaceship   a large planet   landed safely   stepped out
> looked around   walked slowly   huge rocks
> explored   towards a hill   climbed
> looked down   deep, green valley   shock and surprise
> a huge, red building   higher than   wider than
> to get a closer look   crept towards   hid behind
> suddenly I saw   aliens   strange creatures   different colours

Adventure in Space

Using Words

Language

 Write the correct word.

1. The lamb _____ (chirps, grunts, bleats) when it sees its mother.
2. The lion _____ (roars, shouts, barks) when it is angry.
3. The horse _____ (hisses, neighs, howls) when it sees the farmer.
4. The baby _____ (grunts, cries, hums) when it is hungry.
5. The dog _____ (crows, purrs, barks) when it sees a stranger.
6. The cat _____ (grunts, lows, purrs) when it is happy.
7. The wolf _____ (sings, howls, whistles) when it wants food.
8. The bear _____ (barks, croaks, growls) when it is angry.

B **Write the correct word.**

1. A farmer lives in a _____. (barn, farmhouse, pen)
2. A soldier lives in a _____. (barn, shed, barracks)
3. A sailor lives on a _____. (ship, farm, campsite)
4. A queen lives in a _____. (cottage, palace, cave)
5. A monk lives in a _____. (library, monastery, palace)
6. A camper lives in a _____. (office, aeroplane, tent)
7. A prisoner lives in a _____. (cell, tent, mansion)
8. A lighthouse keeper lives in a _____. (castle, lighthouse, barn)

 Make a new word from each word below. Not all letters need to be used.

farmer	_____	replied	_____
Africa	_____	wondered	_____
heard	_____	walked	_____
money	_____	pleased	_____
honest	_____	present	_____

39

Reading

 A Read the story.

Snowflake

Morgan was a magician. She wore a long black cloak, white gloves and a tall, shiny hat.

She knew how to do many clever tricks. Her favourite trick was when she took off her tall top hat, waved it in the air, and then pulled out a fluffy, white rabbit.

Snowflake, the rabbit, had a coat of pure white fur and little pink eyes. Morgan loved her, and trained her to do many funny tricks.

One day, Morgan was doing her tricks at a children's party. She made playing cards disappear and water turn red and blue. The children clapped with delight.

When the time came for Morgan's last trick, there was a great hush. She took off her black hat and showed the children that it was empty. She waved it in the air. Then she put her hand inside for Snowflake.

But she was not there. The hat was still empty.

Morgan was surprised. She shook the hat, turned it upside down, but there was no sign of the rabbit.

The children went home disappointed and Morgan was very sad.

"Snowflake, where are you?" she called, as she searched everywhere.

The days went by, and still Snowflake did not appear.

"I shall just have to do my old tricks with my coloured handkerchiefs," she said.

Morgan remembered that the handkerchiefs were stored in a wooden box in the garage. She went to the garage and found the box. She put her hand inside and felt for the silk handkerchiefs. She touched soft fur.

Quickly, she looked into the box. Staring at her were two big, pink eyes.

"Snowflake!" she cried with joy.

Then Morgan saw eight more eyes! She thought it must be some magic trick and looked closer. Snowflake smiled and showed Morgan her four baby rabbits. Morgan was delighted.

"I always knew you were the best rabbit in the world," she said.

As time went by, the little rabbits showed themselves to be every bit as clever as their mother. Soon, they, too, appeared in Morgan's show.

Once again, Morgan was a very happy magician.

40

Activities

A Answer these questions.

1. Who was Morgan?
2. How was she dressed?
3. What was her favourite trick?
4. What was the name of her pet rabbit?
5. What tricks did Morgan perform at the party?
6. Why were the children disappointed?
7. Why was Morgan very sad?
8. Where did she keep her coloured handkerchiefs?
9. What did she touch in the box?
10. What happened to the baby rabbits?

B Unscramble these sentences.

1. black wore Morgan a long coat.
   _____

2. fluffy a She pulled white out rabbit.
   _____

3. made Morgan red blue water turn and.
   _____

4. no was There sign Snowflake of.
   _____

5. were handkerchiefs The box wooden stored in a.
   _____

6. were as rabbits The baby Snowflake clever as.
   _____

C How many small words can you make from 'handkerchiefs'?

_____ _____ _____
_____ _____ _____
_____ _____ _____
_____ _____ _____

41

Phonics

Consonant Diagraphs: 'ph', 'wh' and 'th'

A Write the missing **f** or **ph** in each word.

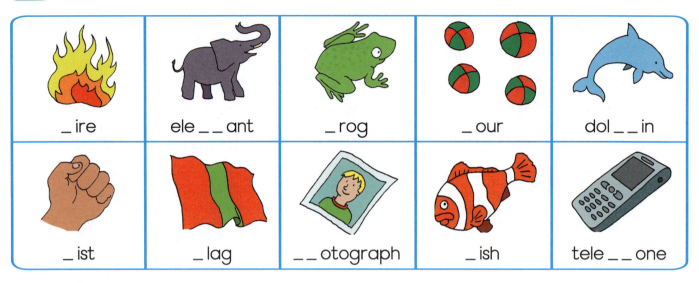

_ ire | ele _ _ ant | _ rog | _ our | dol _ _ in
_ ist | _ lag | _ _ otograph | _ ish | tele _ _ one

B Write questions for each **wh** word. Remember the question mark.

1. Why   <u>did you eat the last bun?</u>
2. When   _____
3. Who   _____
4. Where _____
5. What   _____
6. Which _____

C Write the missing letters for the **th** words. (The letters are jumbled.)

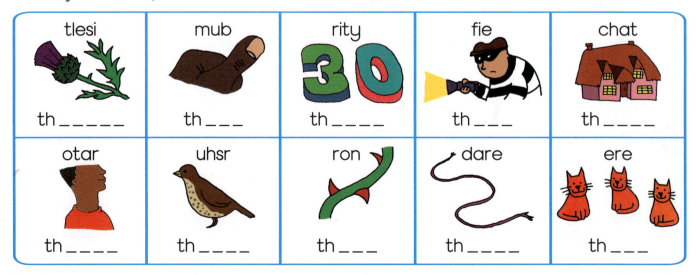

tlesi — th _ _ _ _ _
mub — th _ _ _
rity — th _ _ _ _
fie — th _ _ _
chat — th _ _ _ _
otar — th _ _ _ _
uhsr — th _ _ _ _
ron — th _ _ _
dare — th _ _ _ _
ere — th _ _ _

Grammar

Alphabetical Order

 A Write these words in alphabetical order.

> When words have the same first letter, we look at the second letter.

1. brat, bend, blow. _bend, blow, brat_
2. fish, fry, fox. _____
3. trick, told, tan. _____
4. climb, chant, calm, circle. _____
5. island, ivory, inside, idea. _____
6. reduce, radio, rhyme, rock, ring. _____
7. squelch, shower, screen, saw. _____
8. why, watch, wind, wrap, wear. _____
9. dress, doctor, dish, daffodil. _____
10. hunt, house, help, hammer, hill. _____

 B Write these words in alphabetical order. Match them to their meanings.

dolphin	_carol_	a small thin sharp piece of wood
emerald	_____	a Christmas song
stream	_____	an animal with black and white stripes
carol	_____	food for horses and farm animals
splinter	_____	an animal that lives in the sea
shed	_____	a bird of prey
velvet	_____	a small hut
falcon	_____	a green gem
zebra	_____	a small river
fodder	_____	a kind of thick, soft material

Writing

A Write the start of a story. Use the words below to help you write.

staying   cousins   country   house
set out together   across the fields   a fine, sunny day
laughing   joking   through the woods   came to a pathway
a rusty old gate   creaked loudly   overgrown garden
tall, dark building   broken windows   open door   entered
as quiet as mice   hall   dust on the   cobwebs on the
big stairs   stepped softly   then we heard

The Old House

_____
_____
_____
_____
_____

What happened next? Finish the story yourself.

Language

Using Words

Addressing an envelope

- The name of the person goes on the first line.
- The number of the house and name of the road on the second line.
- The name of the town or village on the third line.
- The name of the county, province, state or region on the fourth line.
- The name of the country on the fifth line.

 Draw envelopes and address them to these people:

1. Yourself.
2. Your best friend.
3. Your mum or dad.
4. Your teacher at your school address.
5. Your brother or sister.
6. Your favourite relative.

Reading

 A Read the story.

The Big Fish

One day, a young Native American boy, named Little Wing, set out to go fishing. He sat in his canoe and paddled off down the river. The river was wide and deep and its waters were clean and clear. Every now and then, Little Wing could see fish swimming over bright rocks down below.

"Today I will catch the big silver fish and bring it to my grandfather," said Little Wing to himself.

The boy loved his grandfather, who was the chief of the tribe. His grandfather was a wise man who knew many things. He knew the names of every star in the night sky. He could whistle the songs of all the birds in the air. He could tell stories that no one else could tell.

His grandfather had told Little Wing where to look for the big silver fish. He paddled away down the river until he came to the place. A big white rock stood out in the rushing water. This rock was where his grandfather always stood to spear fish. Little Wing paddled over to the rock. Taking his own spear into his hands, he climbed onto it. This was the first time he had ever tried to fish alone. Now, he stood in his grandfather's place on the big, white rock in the rushing river.

"Be as still as the rock itself and wait for the fish to come," his grandfather had told him.

Without moving, the boy watched and waited for the big fish. Time passed by, and no fish came. But Little Wing just stood there, as still as the rock.

"Keep your eye on the water, your hand to the spear," his grandfather had said. "And the fish will be yours."

The sun was beginning to sink, but no fish had come. Little Wing's eyes felt tired and his arms felt stiff. Yet, still as a rock, he watched and waited. At last, something moved in the water. The great silver fish had come. It was swimming by the white rock. In a moment, the fish would be gone. Little Wing knew what to do and when to do it. The spear flew from his hand into the rushing water.

That evening, the grandfather ate the fish which Little Wing had caught for him. The old man was very proud of the young boy.

Activities

A Answer these questions.

1. Why did the boy take his canoe down the river?
2. What could he see in the water below?
3. Name three things his grandfather knew.
4. Where was the best place to catch fish?
5. What did the grandfather tell Little Wing to do on the rock?
6. How did the boy catch the fish?
7. What did his grandfather do that evening?
8. Can you guess what kind of fish the boy caught?

B Write the correct word.

1. Little Wing decided to go _____. (diving, filming, fishing)
2. He went down the river in a _____. (raft, dinghy, canoe)
3. His grandfather was _____ (chef, chief, thief) of the tribe.
4. A big _____ (black, wide, white) rock stood out in the river.
5. The spear _____ (grew, flu, flew) from his hand.
6. The grandfather _____ (eight, ate, ape) the fish.

C Make a new word from each word below. Not all letters need to be used.

American _____   whistle _____

canoe _____   spear _____

paddled _____   rushing _____

bright _____   silver _____

tribe _____   ate _____

white _____   proud _____

47

Phonics

Three-letter Blends: 'spl' and 'spr'

 A Write the missing **spl** or **spr** in each word.

___ ead	___ ay	___ int	___ outs
___ inter	___ ash	___ ing	___ atter
___ inter	___ inkle	___ inkler	___ it

 B Match the **spl** or **spr** words to their meaning.

1. spring
2. splinter
3. spray
4. sprinkler
5. spread
6. sprain
7. splendid
8. splutter

A. to have trouble talking because of anger
B. something that's excellent
C. an object that waters the garden (usually)
D. to injure a joint in your body
E. stretch something to its full size
F. to scatter a small amount of liquid
G. a tiny sharp piece of wood (usually)
H. one of the four seasons

Grammar

Comparative and Superlative

A Write the words.

rich	richer	richest
quick	_____	_____
dark	_____	_____
high	_____	_____
clean	_____	_____
big	_____	_____
light	_____	_____
slow	_____	_____

B Write the correct word.

1. My desk is much _____ (cleanest, cleaner) than yours.
2. The sky has got a lot _____ (darker, dark).
3. My bedroom is the _____ (warmer, warmest) in the house.
4. I can jump _____ (high, higher) than my friend.
5. The smallest kitten is very _____ (weaker, weak).
6. The queen is _____ (richest, richer) than the king.
7. The brown dog is the _____ (lazy, laziest).
8. My sister is very _____ (kinder, kind, kindest) to me.
9. The tall clown was the _____ (funny, funniest).
10. My brother's room is _____ (tidiest, tidier) than mine.

Writing

A Write the start of a story. Use the words below to help you write.

> springtime   bright sunshine   birds singing   noticed a robin
> perched on   flew quickly into   followed   an old kettle
> a small, neat nest lined with   five tiny eggs   tiptoed away
> two weeks later   returned five, fluffy chicks
> cheeping and chirping   hungry   busy parents   worms
> visited each day until

The Robin's Nest

_____
_____
_____
_____
_____

What happened next? Finish the story yourself.

Language

Using Words

Writing a letter

The greeting is written on the left-hand side of the page. Note the use of the capital letters.

The writer's full address is at the top right-hand side of the page.

The date should be written a little below the address.

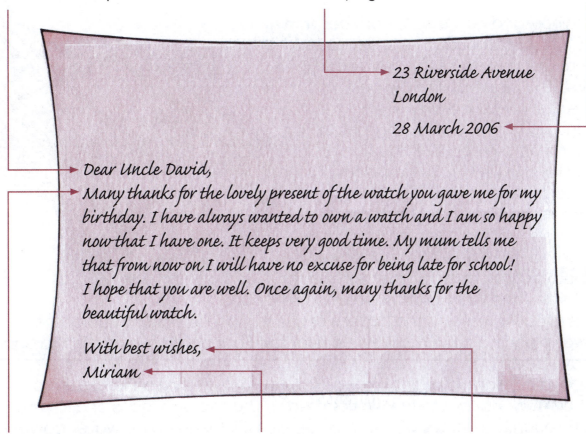

23 Riverside Avenue
London

28 March 2006

Dear Uncle David,
Many thanks for the lovely present of the watch you gave me for my birthday. I have always wanted to own a watch and I am so happy now that I have one. It keeps very good time. My mum tells me that from now on I will have no excuse for being late for school! I hope that you are well. Once again, many thanks for the beautiful watch.

With best wishes,
Miriam

Start on a new line for the message of the letter.

The writer's name should be clearly written beneath the ending.

There are different ways of ending a letter. Examples: Yours faithfully, Kind regards, Yours sincerely.

 A Here are two lists of people. Match them up and write short letters. Example: Write a letter from a vet to a pop-singer!

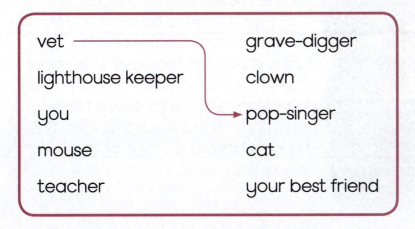

vet — grave-digger
lighthouse keeper — clown
you → pop-singer
mouse — cat
teacher — your best friend

51

Reading

 Read the text.

The First Lighthouse

Over two thousand years ago, work began on the world's first lighthouse. The order to build it came from the King of Egypt. He wanted it to be the first, the biggest, and the best lighthouse the world had ever seen.

Thousands of workers were brought to a small island off the coast of Egypt, where the lighthouse was to be placed. It was to be many years before their work was finished. First, they had to lay down a large square building on which to put the lighthouse tower. When the tower was finished, it stood over 150 metres high. It had eight sides and was built of white marble. At the top of this great tower was the lantern of the lighthouse. And on top of the lantern was placed a huge bronze statue of the Egyptian sun-god. What a sight it must have been!

By day and by night, a bright fire was kept burning in the round lantern of the lighthouse. Wood for the fire was carried to the top by means of a lift which went up through the centre of the tower. It was a lift worked by water power – another invention of the clever Egyptians. However the most brilliant idea of all was the way they used a big mirror to reflect the light from the fire out across the sea. It was said that the light could be seen for forty-five kilometres. During the day, the great white lighthouse was a fine landmark for any sailors at sea. During the night, the powerful beam of light helped to guide ships and to warn them of the rocks along the coast.

Egypt's lighthouse became known all over the ancient world and was listed as one of the Seven Wonders of the World. It stood for almost fifteen hundred years until it was finally destroyed by an earthquake. Sadly, there is hardly a trace of the lighthouse left today.

Activities

A Answer these questions.

1. Where was the lighthouse built?
2. Who ordered it to be built?
3. What was placed on top of the lantern?
4. How was the wood for the fire taken to the top?
5. What was the mirror used for?
6. Why do you think the lighthouse was built of white marble?
7. How long did the building last?
8. What happened to the lighthouse?

B Write **true** or **false**.

1. Work began on the lighthouse over three thousand years ago. _____
2. Hundreds of workers were brought to the island. _____
3. The lighthouse tower stood just under 150 metres high. _____
4. The lighthouse had eight sides. _____
5. There was a lantern on top of the bronze statue. _____
6. The lantern was square shaped. _____
7. The lift went up through the centre of the tower. _____
8. The light could be seen for forty-five miles. _____

C Write the two words each compound word is made from.

lighthouse	=	light	+	house
bedroom	=	_____	+	_____
handbag	=	_____	+	_____
campfire	=	_____	+	_____
homesick	=	_____	+	_____
inside	=	_____	+	_____

53

Phonics

Three-letter Blends: 'scr and 'str'

A Unjumble the letters and complete the **str** words.

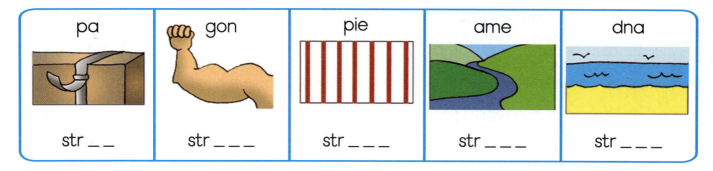

pa	gon	pie	ame	dna
str _ _	str _ _ _	str _ _ _	str _ _ _	str _ _ _

B Unjumble the letters and complete the **scr** words.

we	mea	bu	chat	leibb
scr _ _	scr _ _ _	scr _ _	scr _ _ _ _	scr _ _ _ _ _

C Write the correct word.

1. The sick boy was carried on a _____ (stretcher, scratcher).
2. Did you _____ (strut, scrub) the floor?
3. The _____ (scrap, strap) of her bag has broken.
4. I heard a loud _____ (scream, stream).
5. The man went for a _____ (scroll, stroll) in the park.
6. I turned on my computer _____ (scream, screen).
7. I hold onto the _____ (strong, string) on my kite.
8. My little sister likes to _____ (scribble, struggle) in my book.
9. You can cross the _____ (scream, stream) here.
10. Pick up that _____ (scrap, strap) of paper on the floor.

54

Grammar

Nouns

> A **noun** is the name of **a person** (Ali), **place** (Paris), **animal** (dog), **thing** (table).

A Find the nouns in these sentences and underline them.

1. The cat swam across the wide river.
2. A young child was playing happily in the garden.
3. He gathered nuts and wild strawberries in the woods.
4. Two horses pulled the cart along the street.
5. The wise woman sat in the chair and read a book.
6. He went to New York to visit our aunt.
7. The children watched the goldfish in the bowl.
8. The monkey escaped from his cage in the zoo.
9. The angry girl shouted loudly at the barking dog.
10. The old man walked slowly along the dusty road.

B Write three nouns that belong to each of these groups.

1. Fish _____ _____ _____
2. Dogs _____ _____ _____
3. Countries _____ _____ _____
4. Vegetables _____ _____ _____
5. Cities _____ _____ _____
6. Toys _____ _____ _____
7. Insects _____ _____ _____
8. Fruit _____ _____ _____
9. Flowers _____ _____ _____
10. Sports _____ _____ _____
11. Farm animals _____ _____ _____
12. Capitals _____ _____ _____

Writing

A Write the start of a story. Use the words below to help you write.

> invited to Uncle Jack's farm   packed case   train
> met at the station   tasty supper   bed   rose early
> fed the chickens   collected the eggs   after dinner
> walk up the mountain   wild flowers
> fantastic view   brought down the sheep and lambs
> clever sheepdog   drove sheep into their pens
> following day   cleaned out the stable   fed the horse
> warm and sunny   picnic in the meadow   gathered the hay
> strolled down to the beach   rolling waves   explored rock pools
> late evening   sun sinking   Uncle Jack's stories

A Farm Holiday

What happened next? Finish the story yourself.

Using Words

Language

 A Complete the words.

Farmyard Animals

1. _ oo _ _
2. _ _ mb
3. ch _ _ _
4. _ _ ck
5. h _ _ _ _
6. _ _ _ ke _
7. sh _ _ p _ _ _
8. _ _ _
9. d _ _ _ _ _
10. _ _ _

Reading

 Read the text

The Giraffe

The male giraffe is the tallest animal in the world. He can measure over six metres. A grown man can easily stand upright between his wide front legs. This king of the open bush country lives in Africa.

Giraffes' coats are covered with pretty patterns. The small, bony horns on the top of the head are used for 'neck fighting' with other giraffes. Did you know that giraffes are so tall that the heart is over 60 centimetres long, in order to pump the blood to the top of the head.

It is an amazing sight to see the giraffe plucking the leaves and shoots of the tall acadia tree with his long, black tongue. His thick, hairy lips protect him from prickly thorns and brambles.

Giraffes prefer to sleep standing up so that he can defend himself against attack. A kick from his powerful hind legs could break a man's neck.

The female giraffe gives birth to a single calf. The newborn baby is about one and a half metres tall and at first is very unstable walking on his long legs. The mother nurses and cares for her 'baby'. At the end of the year the young giraffe is strong enough to defend himself. It roams with the rest of the herd, across the open plains of Africa.

Activities

A Answer these questions.

1. In what country does the giraffe live?
2. How tall can the giraffe grow?
3. How is the giraffe's coat covered?
4. What food does the giraffe like to eat?
5. How does the giraffe defend himself against attack?
6. How does the giraffe use the bony horns on the head?
7. Why do giraffes sleep standing up?
8. What is a young giraffe called?
9. How tall is the calf when it's born?
10. Why does the giraffe need a large heart?

B Make a new word from each word below. Not all letters need to be used

giraffe   _____

animal   _____

pump   _____

blood   _____

tongue   _____

upright   _____

attack   _____

herd   _____

roams   _____

plains   _____

Phonics

Soft 'c' and hard 'c'

Soft 'c' (sounds like s) and hard 'c' (sounds like k)

A Write the missing c in each word. Write a sentence for each word on a separate sheet of paper.

_arpet   pen_il   fa_e   _amera   _omb

_ircle   _andle   _igar   _rane   di_e

mi_e   _ream   _amel   _ar   prin_e

B Draw a car in your book, like this:

Write inside it the **hard 'c'** words.

Draw a pencil in your book, like this:

Write inside it the **soft 'c'** words.

1. The _____ is in the cage.
2. I threw the _____ and got six.
3. We put _____ in the salad.
4. Mother lit the _____ .
5. London is a big _____ .
6. Mary put on her _____ .

candle	city
canary	lettuce
dice	necklace

Grammar

Nouns

A Write nouns for these sentences on a separate sheet of paper.

1. The _newsagent_ had sold all the _____ in her shop.
2. _____ walked down the _____ and opened the back _____ .
3. A _____ has four _____ , wags his _____ and barks.
4. _____ hopped on her _____ and cycled to the _____ .
5. The gardener watered the beautiful _____ in her _____ .
6. The thirsty _____ opened the _____ and took a big gulp of _____ .
7. The _____ was dark so the boy turned on the _____ .
8. When the programme was over, _____ turned off the _____ .
9. A tall _____ grew beside the flowing _____ .
10. _____ went on holidays to a foreign _____ last _____ .

B Write lists of nouns on a separate sheet of paper.

boys' names   wild animals   birds

C Find the nouns.

1. The dentist worked in her surgery five days a week.
2. Kim went to the park by bus.
3. The lineswoman raised her flag when the ball went out.
4. Paula sat on the beach making sandcastles.
5. The Amazon is the largest river in the world.
6. Kate rented a DVD from the shop.
7. Norway has lots of snow in winter.
8. A dolphin is a mammal but a shark is a fish.
9. Anna likes to listen to the radio when she is working.
10. The train left Cairo station at midnight.

Writing

A Write a riddle for each animal below.

Example:
I swim in the river.
I swim in the sea.
I have scales on my back.
What can I be?

Answer: *A fish*

1. Elephant

2. Bear

3. Wolf

4. Squirrel

5. Tiger

6. Dog

7. Lion

8. Zebra

Language

Using Words

 A Copy and complete.

Zoo Animals

1. _ _ _ _ ich
2. _ _ nk _ _
3. _ _ _ _ _ _ _ oo
4. t _ _ _ _
5. _ _ ra _ _ _
6. _ _ _ ic _ _
7. _ _ _ ph _ _ _
8. z _ _ _ _
9. _ _ _ l
10. sn _ _ _
11. _ _ m _ _
12. _ ea _

Reading

 A Read the story.

Bell the Cat

For many years, Bell the Cat and lots of mice lived in the same house. The mice were afraid of the cat and they had to be careful all the time.

One day, the mice noticed that the number of mice seemed to be getting smaller all the time, while the cat seemed to be getting fatter. The mice decided to hold a meeting and see what they should do about the cat.

An invitation was sent to every mouse in the house. "Please come to a meeting in the kitchen at twelve o'clock tonight. We need to make a decision as to what we should do about the cat. She is getting very fat lately, and we mice seem to be getting fewer and fewer."

At twelve o'clock that night, the mice gathered around the kitchen table. They all had different ideas as to what should be done about the cat. One mouse said that the owner of the house should sell the cat! Everybody laughed at this! "The owner keeps the cat to get rid of us!" said one young mouse. "We will have to think of something better than that!"

Another young mouse came up with a great idea! "Let us tie a bell around the cat's neck," he said. "Then we will always hear her coming and run out of her way."

Everyone thought that was a marvellous idea! The mice stood up and clapped their paws. They were really delighted until one old mouse called for silence. She stroked her grey whiskers and said, "Which of you will tie the bell round the cat's neck?" Not one single mouse had an answer to that question and one by one, they all left the meeting. Nothing was done about Bell the Cat!

64

Activities

A Write true or false.

1. Bell the cat and a family of mice lived together. _____
2. The mice seemed to be getting fatter. _____
3. The cat decided to hold a meeting. _____
4. An invitation was sent to every mouse in the house. _____
5. The mice gathered around the kitchen table. _____
6. One mouse said the cat should sell the owner. _____
7. They decided to tie a bell around Bell's neck. _____
8. The mice clapped their paws. _____
9. The old mouse stroked her green whiskers. _____
10. Nothing was done about Bell the cat. _____

B Write the correct word.

1. A mouse has four _____. (hooves, paws, ears)
2. A cat eats _____. (nuts, snails, mice)
3. A mouse lives in a _____. (burrow, hole, drey)
4. A cat sleeps during the _____. (winter, night, day)
5. A mouse is bigger than a _____. (cat, tadpole, fox)
6. A cat has no _____. (wings, tail, ears)
7. A mouse's tail is _____. (short, bushy, long)
8. A cat is covered in _____. (fur, spines, scales).

Phonics

Soft 'g' and Hard 'g'

Soft 'g' (as in giant) and hard 'g' (as in gun)

A Write the missing g in each word. Write a sentence for each word.

_ oat   _ lobe   _ iraffe   pa _ e   _ un

_ lass   _ host   bad _ e   _ iant   _ uitar

ca _ e   dra _ on   brid _ e   _ ymnast   ba _

B Copy the table below on a separate sheet of paper. Write each word from **A** in the correct column.

Hard 'g' words	Soft 'g' words
glass	cage

Verbs

Grammar

> A **verb** is an action word (run, walk, read).

 A Write the verbs in these sentences.

1. Maha sent an email to her sister.
2. The playful puppy barked at the cat.
3. The traffic lights turned green.
4. The monkey swung from branch to branch.
5. Tom washed his hair and then combed it.
6. Rajan went to the post office and posted the letter.
7. The men rowed out into the centre of the lake.
8. David painted the garden seat.

B Write verbs for these sentences.

1. The dog _____ Tom on the leg.
2. Kate _____ a big fish in the pond.
3. Hundreds of people _____ the parade.
4. A bear _____ smaller than an elephant.
5. The nurse _____ in the hospital.
6. His train _____ yesterday morning.
7. Anita _____ a great goal.
8. We _____ them outside the church.

 C Write the correct verb.

1. The seagull _____ (glides, hops, walks) over the water.
2. The magpie _____ (crawls, swims, hops) from branch to branch.
3. The eagle _____ (jumps, swoops, stamps) on its prey.
4. The duck _____ (trots, runs, waddles) into the pond.
5. The field mouse _____ (strolls, scampers, gallops) into its nest.
6. The butterfly _____ (hovers, swings, prances) near the flowers.

Writing

A Write the start of a story. Use the words below to help you write.

> hiking all day   mountains   valleys   late afternoon
> edge of a forest   cool, clear stream   a good spot
> pitched the tent   collected firewood   as hungry as a   cooked
> ate a delicious   sun was setting   red sky   tall pines
> crackling log fire   played the guitar   moon appeared
> twinkling star   tired   time for bed   crawled into
> hushed and still   hoot of an owl

The Camp

_____
_____
_____
_____

What happened next? Finish the story yourself.

Using Words

Language

A Write the correct verb.

> crashed   is blowing   flies   fell   swam   will win
> was shining   hopped   broke   was open

1. A plane _____.
2. The fish _____.
3. That horse _____.
4. The frog _____.
5. The wind _____.
6. The car _____.
7. Snow _____.
8. The door _____.
9. The bottle _____.
10. The sun _____.

B Write the correct verb.

1. The lamb _____ (chirps, grunts, bleats) when it sees its mother.
2. The cat _____ (quacks, shouts, hisses) when it is scared.
3. The horse _____ (hisses, neighs, howls) when it sees the farmer.
4. The baby _____ (cries, grunts, hums) when it is hungry.
5. The dog _____ (crows, purrs, barks) when it sees a stranger.
6. The cat _____ (grunts, lows, purrs) when it is happy.
7. The wolf _____ (sings, howls, whistles) when it wants food.
8. The bear _____ (barks, croaks, growls) when it is angry.

C Unscramble the letters in the months of the year.
Do not forget capital letters!

rarefbuy   eocotbr

hamrc   mvonebre

aym   neju

iparl   uaguts

auayjnr   ulyj

reecedmb   remtespeb

Reading

A Read the poem.

The Fairies

1

Up the airy mountain,
Down the rushy glen,
We daren't go a-hunting
for fear of little men;
Wee folk, good folk,
Trooping all together;
Green jacket, red cap,
And white owl's feather!

2

Down along the rocky shore,
some make their home,
They live on crispy pancakes
Of yellow tide-foam;
Some of the reeds
Of the black mountain-lake,
With frogs for their watchdogs,
All night awake.

3

By the craggy hillside,
Through the mosses bare,
They have planted thorn trees
For pleasure, here and there.
Is any man so daring
As dig them up in spite,
He shall find their sharpest thorns
In his bed at night.

4

Up the airy mountain,
Down the rushy glen,
We daren't go a-hunting
for fear of little men;
Wee folk, good folk,
Trooping all together;
Green jacket, red cap,
And white owl's feather!

William Allingham

Activities

A Write **true** or **false**.

1. The wee folk wore green caps. _____
2. Some made their home along the sandy shore. _____
3. Some folk had frogs as watchdogs. _____
4. The wee folk planted holly trees. _____
5. They planted trees for pleasure. _____
6. The wee folk wore green jumpers. _____

B Make a new word from each word below.

down	_____	pancakes	_____
hunting	_____	crispy	_____
trooping	_____	mountain	_____
feather	_____	thorn	_____
jacket	_____	pleasure	_____

C Unscramble these sentences.

1. dare We not hunting go.
2. wee The folk on live pancakes crispy.
3. live folk Some wee the in reeds.
4. wee The folk as frogs have watchdogs.
5. planted They thorn by the trees hillside craggy.
6. folk wee The green wear jackets caps and red.

Phonics

Silent Letters: 'k' and 'w'

A Write each **silent k** word.

1. You tie one of these. kn _ _
2. A joint in your finger. kn _ _ _ _ _ _
3. A joint in your leg. kn _ _
4. Make clothing from wool. kn _ _
5. Hit. kn _ _ _
6. Rest on your knees. kn _ _ _
7. _ _ _ _ _ and fork. kn _ _ _
8. Understand something. kn _ _

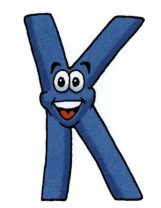

B Write the missing **silent w** words.

| wrong | wreath | write | wrist | wren | wrap | answer |
| wrench | sword | wriggle | wrinkles | wrestle |

1. I always _____ my homework neatly.
2. The _____ slipped and the mechanic hurt his _____ .
3. The pirate was armed with a _____ .
4. The worm began to _____ on the soil.
5. The _____ to that question is _____ .
6. The old man had _____ on his face.
7. The _____ is a tiny bird.
8. She placed a _____ on the grave.
9. Get paper to _____ the present.
10. The strong men did not _____ for long.

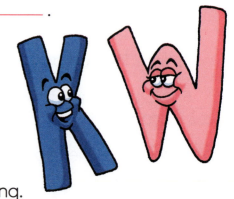

Verbs

Grammar

 A Find the verbs in these sentences.

1. The children posted the letters.
2. The bus will leave at seven o'clock.
3. The puppy is eating the meat.
4. They slept in a shed near the river.
5. Meera was reading a book in the library.
6. The phone rang in the hall.
7. A small bird flew into the bush.
8. Owls usually come out at night.

B Use a verb to finish each sentence.

1. The brave girl _____ .
2. A kind old man _____ .
3. Two strong horses _____ .
4. A huge army _____ .
5. The clever boy _____ .
6. The ugly duckling _____ .
7. A mean thief _____ .
8. The rusty old car _____ .
9. The rugby team _____ .
10. Her jealous sister _____ .

 C Write the correct verb.

falls	neighs	gurgles	blows	waddles	hoots	rises
	barks		brays	purrs		

1. The owl _____ .
2. The baby _____ .
3. The wind _____ .
4. The sun _____ .
5. The rain _____ .
6. The duck _____ .
7. The dog _____ .
8. The cat _____ .
9. The horse _____ .
10. The donkey _____ .

73

Writing

 A Write the start of a story. Use the words below to help you write.

> on the hillside   rainbow   followed   across   over   through
> a field of bright flowers   a hawthorn tree   something flashed
> discovered a crock of gold   grabbed coins   filled my pockets
> heard a noise   turned   sitting on a   he wore a   jacket
> trousers   shoes   seemed angry because

The Fairies

What happened next? Finish the story yourself.

Using Words

Language

A Write the **odd word out** in each list below.

1. seal, sheep, skunk, rabbit, squirrel.
2. pike, trout, whale, herring, cod.
3. rabbit, badger, fox, hare, frog.
4. peach, pineapple, pear, potato, plum.
5. oyster, mussel, octopus, limpet, whelk.
6. tiger, kangeroo, lion, elephant.
7. magpie, penguin, cuckoo, robin, blackbird.
8. stallion, mare, buffalo, foal, pony.
9. Husky, St Bernard, Alsatian, Siamese.

B Unscramble the letters of the last word. Write the correct words.

1. The car is in the **gearga**.
2. The room in the top storey of the house is called the **ictta**.
3. A tame rabbit lives in a **chtuh**.
4. The home in which a snail lives is called a **llesh**.
5. A small house in the country is called a **octtega**.
6. A house which stands apart on its own is **deacthde**.
7. When people go camping they sleep in **settn**.
8. Stone Age people lived in **scvae**.

C How many small words can you make from 'pineapple'?

Reading

 A Read the text.

The Shy Kingfisher

The brightly-coloured kingfisher is called a 'flying jewel'. This is because it has a coat of brilliant blue, green and orange colours. It lives near rivers, streams and lakes. The kingfisher's nest is built at the end of a long narrow tunnel, dug under a sandy bank or stream. The tunnel can be up to two metres long. The nest is made from fish bones. During the breeding season, the female lays between two and eight shiny white eggs, which hatch after three weeks.

Both parents take care of the baby birds. They feed them on a diet of fish, insects and small eels. At the first sign of danger, the young kingfishers run backwards up the tunnel. When they are strong enough, they are chased out of the nest by their parents. The young then begin to fish for themselves and live in a new part of the river bank. Birds of prey, like the hawk, seldom attack kingfishers because they don't like their smell.

The kingfisher is excellent at fishing. It perches on a low branch overhanging the water and waits patiently for its prey to come along. As soon as it spots a fish, it plunges its red dagger-shaped bill into it. The speared fish is lifted out of the water and swallowed. Later on, they throw up the digested fish to feed their young.

The kingfisher may have as many as three broods in a breeding season.

Activities

A Answer these questions.

1. Why is the kingfisher called a 'flying jewel'?
2. Where does it build its nest?
3. How long does it take the eggs to hatch?
4. What do the young birds eat?
5. Why are kingfishers rarely attacked by hawks?
6. How do the parents feed their young?
7. Write each of these words in an interesting sentence: hopped, glided, swooped.
8. Describe the kingfisher's nest.

B Write true or false.

1. The kingfisher's feathers are brown. _____
2. Kingfishers live near the sea. _____
3. Kingfishers make their nests from fish bones. _____
4. Kingfisher eggs are white. _____
5. Only the female kingfisher looks after the baby birds. _____
6. Kingfishers catch fish with their claws. _____

C Write the missing words.

> stream   hatch   fish   jewel   parents   eight   fishing
> tunnel   plunges   three

The kingfisher is called a flying _____ . It builds its nest at the end of a narrow _____ under a sandy bank or _____ . The female lays between two and _____ eggs which _____ after _____ weeks. Both _____ take care of the baby birds. The kingfisher is excellent at _____ . As soon as it spots a _____ it _____ its bill into it.

Phonics

Root Words and Compound Words

> Root words (small words) and Compound words.
> rain (root word) + drop (root word) = raindrop (compound word)

A Ring the root words in these compound words. Write them out.

1. (camp)fire = __camp__ + __fire__
2. seaside = _____ + _____
3. toothbrush = _____ + _____
4. sunflower = _____ + _____
5. rainbow = _____ + _____
6. blackberry = _____ + _____
7. moonlight = _____ + _____
8. birthday = _____ + _____
9. racehorse = _____ + _____
10. headache = _____ + _____

B Match the root words. Write the compound word they make.

butter	shoe	_____
horse	room	_____
basket	noon	_____
grass	fly	_____
after	ball	_____
class	hopper	_____

ball	keeper	_____
goal	be	_____
may	way	_____
run	mark	_____
book	room	_____

Grammar

Adjectives

> Adjectives are words that tell us more about nouns.
> Examples: an angry tiger, a huge giant, a sly fox.

 A Write the correct adjective to describe each face.

| angry | old | young | bald | happy | sad |

happy _____ _____ _____ _____ _____

 B Underline the adjectives.

1. The big dog saw the brown rat.
2. The pretty butterfly landed on the red rose.
3. The grey squirrel cracked a hard nut.
4. The gentle lamb played in the green field.
5. The rich man bought a large car.
6. The timid mouse ate the fresh cheese.
7. The grizzly bear lived in the deep woods.
8. The sly fox ate a plump duck.
9. The black beetle crawled under a mossy stone.
10. The small, black horse drank the clear water.

 C Write an adjective for each noun below.

Writing

A Write the start of a story. Use the words below to help you write.

> out walking   friends   picnic   trees rustling   crashing noise
> looked up towards the sky   dark shadow   huge dinosaur
> enormous   terrified   friends ran   stamping the ground

Dinosaur Adventure

_____
_____
_____
_____
_____

What happened next? Finish the story yourself.

Language

Using Words

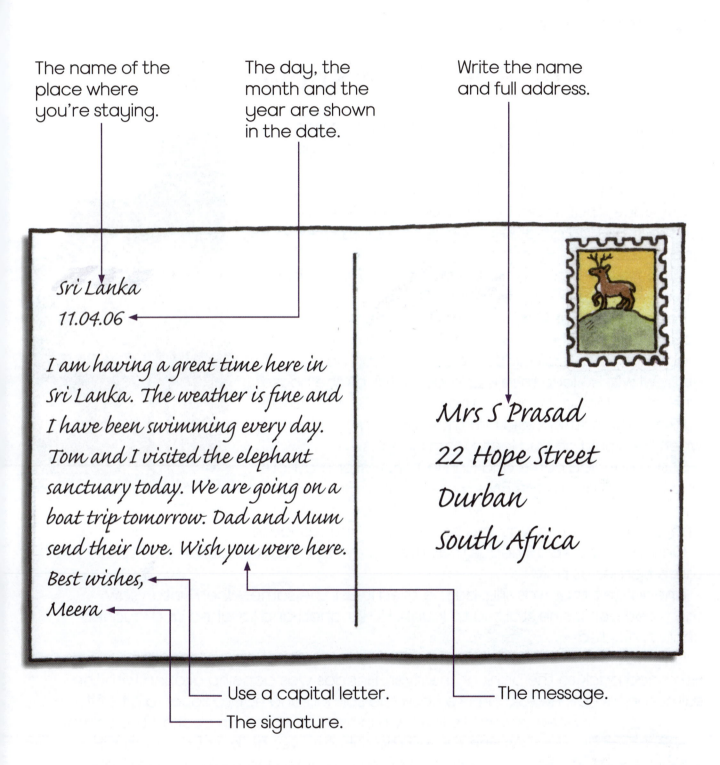

The name of the place where you're staying.

The day, the month and the year are shown in the date.

Write the name and full address.

Sri Lanka
11.04.06

I am having a great time here in Sri Lanka. The weather is fine and I have been swimming every day. Tom and I visited the elephant sanctuary today. We are going on a boat trip tomorrow. Dad and Mum send their love. Wish you were here.
Best wishes,
Meera

Mrs S Prasad
22 Hope Street
Durban
South Africa

Use a capital letter.
The signature.
The message.

A You are staying on Mars. Write a postcard to your friend back home.

Reading

 A Read the story.

The Salmon of Knowledge

Long ago in Ireland, there lived a wise man named Finegas. Finegas knew that he would never be really wise until he caught Fintan.

Fintan was an old salmon known as the Salmon of Knowledge, that swam in the River Boyne. It was said that he had great knowledge of things past and present.

For seven years, Finegas tried to catch Fintan, but the salmon was always too clever for him.

Poor old Finegas began to think that he would never catch Fintan. Sometimes when the thought of this made him really sad, he'd sit by his fire and howl. His howl was so loud that it carried as far as the house where Finn McCool was staying with his foster mothers.

His foster mothers told him that the day would come when he would go and learn from Finegas.

Soon that day came and Finn left his foster mothers and headed off for the River Boyne. When Finn reached the river, he found Finegas sitting on the bank, fishing. Finn told him who he was and he became Finegas' pupil.

One day, Finn told Finegas that the best way to catch salmon was to use three berries as bait.

Finegas felt that was silly, but he tried it just the same. When Fintan saw the three berries he started to laugh. He laughed and laughed and laughed until . . . he died!

Finn was in the woods collecting wood when he heard a yell from Finegas. He raced back to the bank of the river. Finegas was dancing around with the salmon in his net. He told Finn to cook the salmon and not to touch a bit of it.

Finegas went to lie down in his hut, while Finn cooked the salmon. As Finn turned the salmon over he burnt his thumb. He stuck his thumb in his mouth and sucked it. No sooner had he done that than he began to feel very strange.

He brought the salmon to Finegas, but as soon as Finegas saw Finn he knew what had happened. He told Finn that he may as well eat the rest of the salmon.

Finn sat down and finished the salmon. From that day on whenever he wanted to know anything, all he had to do was suck his thumb.

Activities

A Answer these questions.

1. Where did Finegas live?
2. What was Fintan?
3. How long had Finegas been trying to catch Fintan?
4. What did Finegas do when he was sad?
5. Where was Finn McCool staying?
6. What did Finegas use as bait?
7. What was Finn doing when Finegas caught the salmon?
8. What happened to Finn when he was cooking?
9. What did Finn do with the rest of the salmon?
10. What happened after that whenever Finn sucked his thumb?

B Write true or false.

1. Long ago there lived a wise man named Vinegar. _____
2. Fintan was the Salmon of Knowledge. _____
3. Fintan had been trying to catch Finegas for seven years. _____
4. Sometimes Finegas sat by his fire and hid. _____
5. Finn was staying with his foster mothers. _____
6. Finegas used three berries to catch Finn. _____
7. Fintan laughed and laughed until he cried. _____
8. Finn burnt the salmon. _____

C Unscramble these sentences. Do not forget capital letters and full stops!

1. swam of the river the salmon in knowledge boyne
2. salmon always clever too finegas was for the
3. finegas fire would by howl sit the and
4. finn collecting was woods in some the wood
5. dancing salmon in finegas his was net with around the
6. cook finegas finn salmon told to the
7. ate rest finn the salmon the of

83

Phonics

Syllables

A Find the **root** word of the compound words below

helpful	thankful	brightest
smallest	freshest	rocking
careless	useless	cupful
wishful	likeness	sadness
boldness	walking	darkness

B Copy each word into your book. Divide it into two syllables.

Example: write **tennis** as **ten/nis**.

tennis	sudden	carrot	rubber	summer
rabbit	winner	tunnel	butter	lesson
happen	kitten	puppet	pepper	supper

C Match the syllables. Write the words

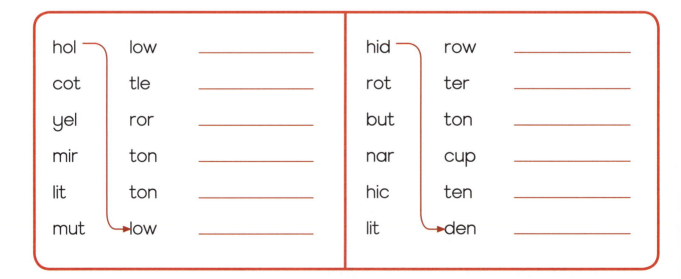

Grammar

Adjectives

A Write adjectives for these nouns.

1. The _____ child sat beside the _____ fire.
2. The _____ wolf escaped into the _____ forest.
3. The _____ balloon burst with a _____ bang.
4. A _____ beggar leaned against the _____ door.
5. All the lambs were sold by the _____ farmer.
6. The _____ explorer sailed away in a _____ ship.
7. The _____ train rumbled into the _____ station.
8. The field was covered with _____ flowers.
9. We sat under a _____ tree and had a _____ picnic.
10. The firefighter made his way through the _____ smoke and flames.

B Write six adjectives for each of these nouns.

House	Tiger	Puppy
1. _____	_____	_____
2. _____	_____	_____
3. _____	_____	_____
4. _____	_____	_____
5. _____	_____	_____
6. _____	_____	_____

C Write pairs of adjectives for each of these nouns.

1. A _____ , _____ giant.
2. The _____ , _____ water.
3. The _____ , _____ desert.
4. A _____ , _____ kitten.
5. A _____ , _____ fox.
6. The _____ , _____ wall.
7. A _____ , _____ cake.
8. The _____ , _____ vet.

85

Writing

A Write the start of a story. Use the words bellow to help you write

> summer   fair   Mum and Dad   Meg and Tom   stalls
> dodgem cars   ghost train   big wheel   tickets
> higher and higher   tightly   reached the top   see for miles
> something strange happened   big wheel stopped   frightened

The Big Wheel

_____
_____
_____
_____
_____
_____

What happened next? Finish the story yourself.

Language

Using Words

A Write the correct word.

| mouse | sheep | horse | nest | tadpole | kid |
| dog | hutch | wing | duckling | | |

1. Duck is to _____ as sheep is to lamb.
2. Bird is to _____ as spider is to web.
3. Caterpillar is to butterfly as _____ is to frog.
4. Kitten is to cat as puppy is to _____ .
5. Horse is to stable as rabbit is to _____ .
6. Paw is to dog as hoof is to _____ .
7. Shoal is to herring as flock is to _____ .
8. Spider is to fly as cat is to _____ .
9. _____ is to bird as fin is to fish.
10. _____ is to goat as calf is to elephant.

B Write the correct word.

| bravely | sweetly | loudly | easily | slowly | carefully |
| heavily | angrily | | | | |

1. The soldier fought _____ but in the end he had to surrender.
2. The boat moved _____ against the strong tide.
3. Mina sang _____ at the school concert.
4. The policeman knocked _____ on the door.
5. The old woman walked _____ on the dusty road.
6. Kate was _____ the best pupil in the class.
7. The farmer spoke _____ to the boys.
8. The postman walked _____ up the footpath.

Reading

A Read the text.

Dolphins

Dolphins live in the sea but they are mammals, not fish. This means that they give birth to live young, rather than laying eggs like fish, and the mother dolphin feeds her young with milk from her body. Like other mammals, dolphins have lungs and breathe air. In fact, they must come to the surface once or twice every minute in order to take a breath. Dolphins breathe through the hole in the top of their head, which is called a blowhole.

Dolphins are known for being very clever animals and many scientists believe that dolphins are one of the most intelligent animals in the world.

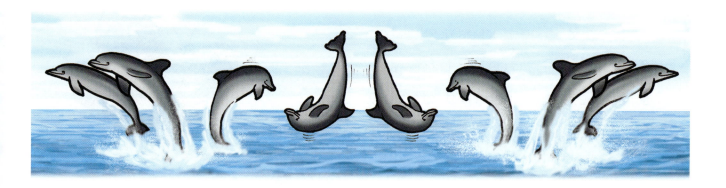

The bottle-nosed dolphin is probably the best-known type of dolphin. Its short, upturned beak makes it look like it is smiling. Bottle-nosed dolphins are grey all over, but their backs are a darker shade than their undersides. Bottle-nosed dolphins live in warm, shallow waters and usually stay quite close to land.

The other well-known type of dolphin is the common dolphin. This dolphin has a dark band around its eyes, which spreads to the end of its long, narrow beak. Common dolphins have black backs, white undersides, and grey and brown stripes on their sides. They can sometimes be found swimming in large groups, called 'schools', and they are often seen in the open ocean.

Both bottle-nosed and common dolphins like to swim alongside ships. As they do so, they may leap out of the water and turn somersaults. Since ancient times, many sailors have believed that seeing a dolphin is lucky. They think that if they see a dolphin near the ship, it means the voyage will go well and they will return home safely.

Activities

A Write **true** or **false**.

1. Dolphins are fish, not mammals. _____
2. Dolphins must come to the surface to breathe. _____
3. The bottle-nosed dolphin looks like it is smiling. _____
4. The bottle-nosed dolphin is brown. _____
5. Common dolphins are often seen in the open ocean. _____
6. Dolphins like to swim alongside ships. _____
7. Many sailors believe that seeing a dolphin is unlucky. _____
8. The common dolphin has a dark band around its eyes. _____

B Unscramble these sentences. Do not forget capital letters and full stops.

1. dolphins the in sea live
2. lungs breathe dolphins and air have
3. stay dolphins close bottle-nosed to land
4. swim dolphins in schools common
5. many think dolphins sailors lucky are
6. very are dolphins intelligent

Phonics

Syllables

A Copy each word into your book. Divide it into two syllables.

Example: write **silly** as **sil/ly**.

silly	crazy	jelly	fifty
rusty	handy	forty	holly
sixty	cozy	nappy	chilly
angry	messy	candy	grumpy
happy	jolly	ugly	clumsy

B Join the syllables. Write the words.

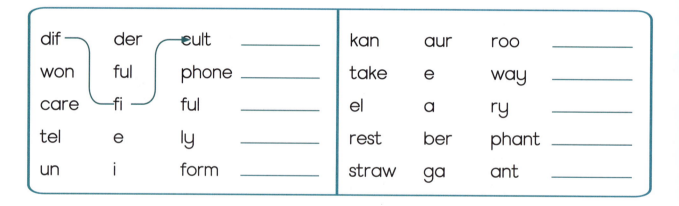

dif	der	cult	_____	kan	aur	roo	_____
won	ful	phone	_____	take	e	way	_____
care	fi	ful	_____	el	a	ry	_____
tel	e	ly	_____	rest	ber	phant	_____
un	i	form	_____	straw	ga	ant	_____

C Write a list of the two syllable and three syllable words.

rabbit takeaway dragon holly elephant blackberry butter some body tummy el grumpy dirty angry terrible general

Grammar

Confusing Words

A Write **two, too** or **to**.

Examples: I have **two** pups **to** bring **to** the vet.
I have **two** pups **too**.

1. They have _____ televisions sets in their house.
2. The _____ boys cycled _____ the seaside.
3. It is _____ early _____ go _____ bed.
4. Early _____ bed and early _____ rise, makes one healthy, wealthy and wise.
5. The child was _____ excited _____ sleep.
6. I am going _____ the pictures with my _____ friends.
7. The _____ lambs loved _____ play with their mother.
8. The teacher spoke _____ the _____ boys in the last row.
9. There were _____ many people trying _____ get into the hall.
10. The problem was _____ difficult _____ solve.

B Write **its** or **it's** (it is).

Examples: The bird is in **its** nest. **It's** a lovely day.

1. _____ raining outside.
2. The hedgehog's spines protect it from _____ enemies.
3. The car rolled over on _____ side.
4. _____ going to be a fine day.
5. The cuckoo left _____ egg in the other bird's nest.
6. My pet cat hurt _____ front paw.
7. The meat has lost _____ flavour.
8. _____ a long way to Antarctica.
9. The ostrich is proud of _____ feathers.
10. _____ better late than never.

Writing

A Write the start of a story. Use the words bellow to help you write.

> bored   friends   orchard   ripe apples   nobody around
> climbed   picked   lost balance   fell off   a sharp, piercing pain
> broken   in agony

A Bad Fall

_____
_____
_____
_____

What happened next? Finish the story yourself.

Language

Using Words

A Write the correct word.

| marched   dived   sneaked   wriggled   swung   ran |
| waddled   trotted |

1. The swallow _____ into the barn.
2. The fox _____ into the chicken coop.
3. The worm _____ along the ground.
4. The duck _____ across the road.
5. The pony _____ around the race track.
6. The monkey _____ from branch to branch.
7. The dog _____ out of the door.
8. The soldier _____ up the road.

B Write the correct word.

1. A lion has four _____ (hooves, tusks, paws).
2. A lion _____ (barks, roars, bellows).
3. A lioness has no _____ (tail, mane, claws).
4. A lion is smaller than an _____ (ant, elephant, otter).
5. A young lion is called a _____ (puppy, kitten, cub).
6. A lion cannot _____ (swim, leap, fly).
7. A lion lives in a _____ (coop, hole, den).
8. A lion has a covering of _____ (skin, wool, spines).

C Unscramble the letters to find members of the cat family.

1. ilno _____
2. gtrei _____
3. dlproae _____
4. hheecta _____
5. rgjaau _____
6. xynl _____
7. muap _____
8. nhprtea _____

Reading

A Read the story.

Strange Friends

A stork and a fox were once very close friends. However, the stork never really trusted the fox, because she knew foxes were known to be sly.

One day, the fox invited the stork to a meal. "My den is on the edge of the wood," he said. "It is under a large beech tree on the bank of the river. You can't miss it!"

They fixed a date and the stork arrived in good time for the evening meal. "Just choose what you like to eat," said the fox. "Don't be afraid to taste things you are not sure about!"

However, when she sat down to eat, the stork was shocked to find that the food had been served on huge shallow plates and was made up of different soups. Her long bill could not pick up one drop of soup. At the same time, the fox was lapping away at his ease until he had finished the lot!

The stork said nothing, but made up her mind to get her own back.

"I would like you to have tea with me next week," she told the fox. "You know where I live. Look for a clump of weeds near the bank of the lake. My nest is in the middle. I'll expect you at sundown!"

The fox ate very little on the day he was going to visit the stork. When they sat down to the meal, the stork served all the food in tall narrow glasses, and the angry fox was not able to get his tongue to the food. He never ate a bite, but what could he say? He had got just what he deserved!

Activities

A Write the correct word.

1. A _____ (stoat, stork, sparrow) and a fox were close friends.
2. The fox was known to be _____ (shy, slow, sly).
3. The stork was invited to a _____ (meat, team, meal).
4. My den is under a _____ (beach, beech, bean) tree.
5. The food was served on _____ (shallow, sparrow, sharp) plates.
6. Her long _____ (ball, bell, bill) couldn't pick up the soup.
7. The fox _____ (laughed, lapped, landed) at his ease.
8. The food was in tall _____ (narrow, tunnel, shallow) glasses.

B Unscramble the following words.

1. wrohvee
2. drairve
3. sturdet
4. wallosh
5. ohoesc
6. cheskdo
7. veesrdde
8. dishfine

Reading

A Read the poem.

If I Knew

If I knew the box where the smiles are kept,
No matter how large the key,
Or strong the bolt I would try so hard
'Twould open I know for me,
Then over the land and sea I'd cast,
The smiles to romp and play,
That the children's faces might hold them fast
For many and many a day.

If I knew the box that was large enough
To hold all the frowns I meet,
I would like to gather them every one
From the nursery, school or street,
Then, folding and holding, I'd pack them in
And turning the monster key,
I'd hire a giant to drop the box
To the depths of the deep, deep sea.

Anonymous